"In sharing pieces of herself, Kristen Costello holds up a mirror to the reader's inner self as well. Wrapped in beautiful yet digestible imagery, you'll be enthralled by *Tidal Pools and Other Small Infinities*. You'll walk away with more gratitude for the slow burn of the healing process. Reading this book was like watching an intricate magic trick unfold. How does Costello do it?"

— Alicia Cook, author of *Sorry I Haven't Texted You Back*

"*Tidal Pools and Other Small Infinities* feels like you are walking into a new season filled with the kind of hope and beauty you didn't know you needed. It is gentle like a new beginning and takes you to a place that feels like home. It will open your heart in all of the ways that feel safe while reminding you that you're exactly where you are meant to be."

— Wilder, author of *nocturnal* and *golden*

"*Tidal Pools and Other Small Infinities* is a heartfelt, honest collection about what it's like to see forever with someone else, then learn to face infinity on your own. Tied together with beautiful imagery you can almost touch, Costello's writing will help you move forward."

— Shelby Leigh, author of *Girl Made of Glass*

"Through poignant introspection, *Tidal Pools and Other Small Infinities* examines how life's smallest moments can often be its most significant. Honest and heart-wrenching with threads of innocence, resilience, and hope throughout, Costello's collection takes readers on a journey through not just falling in love, but—falling in love with oneself. The book rises like a phoenix from its own ashes. A must read for anyone looking to realize their own infinity."

— Michelle Awad, author of *Soul Trash, Space Garbage*

"*Tidal Pools and Other Small Infinities* is a tender exploration of love—where it begins, how it falls apart, and who we become in the aftermath. Through dreamy language and gentle imagery Kristen Costello reminds us that no matter how deep we find ourselves in waves of sadness, there is beauty waiting for us on the other side of it."

— Caitlin Conlon, author of *The Surrender Theory*

tidal pools
and other small infinities

kristen costello

central
avenue

2023

Published by Central Avenue Poetry, an imprint of Central Avenue Marketing Ltd.
www.centralavenuepublishing.com

TIDAL POOLS AND OTHER SMALL INFINITIES

Trade Paperback: 978-1-77168-356-2
EPUB: 978-1-77168-357-9

Published in Canada
Printed in United States of America

1. POETRY / Women   2. POETRY / Subjects & Themes - Nature

1 3 5 7 9 10 8 6 4 2

Keep up with Central Avenue

to all the seekers

praise   i

tidal pools   1

beginning

ivy   4

i want to know you   5

edge   6

dinner dance   7

first date   8

careless/carefree   9

scenic route   10

thaw   11

rendezvous   12

preservation   13

three wishes   14

the sound of you   15

trajectory   16

storm chaser   17

the thief   18

the wanderers   19

daylight savings   20

multicolored envy   21

sidewalks in june   22

driveway   23

theme park   24

beachcombing   25

jetty days   26

musings on muses   27

intricacy   28

game nights   29

the theory of us   30

durability   31

the pantry: top shelf   32

small comforts   33

friday nights   34

last wednesday   35

our talks   36

idols and mortals   37

ending

night fear   40

atlantic   41

breaths   42

nightstand notebook   43

premonition   44

fog   46

the knot   47

projectiles and persistence   48

urge   49

follow the leader   50

stomach this   51

friendly fire   52

ashen evening   53

sugar-free   54

measured   55

mummy   56

a daydreamed dimension   57

another night   58

the fading   59

endings   60

barren   61

favorites   62

unknowns   63

rationalization   64

passed   65

space   66

absence   67

invasion   69

farsighted   71

waste   72

entertainment   74

betrayal   75

useless charms   76

enemies   77

tantrums   78

jealousy   79

last word   80

peaches   81

habits   82

expectations   83

dim   84

resignation   85

lost interests   86

reprieve   87

insomnia   88

muffled   89

rush hour   90

beginning (again)

the drive home   92

hushed   93

subplot   94

she   95

blank calendar   97

ventriloquism   98

onward   99

stepping into the light   100

sparks   101

flight   102

exile   103

power   104

moon   105

author   106

resurrection   107

beginnings   108

awakening   109

radical self-acceptance   110

icarus   111

boundless   112

breakaway   113

architecture   114

independence   115

arizona   116

stargazer   117

palate   118

lessons in botany   119

substance   120

clever crown   121

the writer   122

beckoning   123

the sculptor   124

forward   125

acknowledgments   126

about the poet   129

credits   130

tidal pools

I'm comforted
by the fact
there are endless stories
bubbling
beneath the surface –
there's so much
to be learned
from tidal pools
about small infinities
and seeking
deeper.

beginning

ivy

She was a wild thing
always running barefoot
through the forest
leaving fairy-footprints
in the dirt.

She kept her Spanish moss hair
unpinned,
stockings in a pile of beige
on the welcome mat.

Is it possible to outrun expectations?

She isn't looking to be tamed –
dragged back to the concrete,
scraped knees shoved in stockings.

She wants unlandscaped love –
two fence-free hearts
following fireflies
deeper and deeper
into the forest.

i want to know you

Whether you're afraid of sharks or spiders,
death or love.

I want to know if it's grammatical errors
that drive you crazy
or the people correcting them,
if you're more comfortable
shaking sand
or snow out of your hair,
if you prefer coffee or tea,
bars or board games.

I want to know which of your friends
you've cried in front of,
if you've ever laughed chocolate milk
out of your nose,
or kissed someone you didn't love.

I want to know you,
the you beneath the layer
of small talk
always kept
shined and smudgeless,

I'm just hoping one day
you'll invite me
in.

e d g e

The day is gray
but the clouds carry anticipation
in the breaths between raindrops.

You taste like cold coffee
and unanswered questions –
there's a prologue
on your tongue.

I am cloaked in cumulus,
cautious and quiet –

lingering
at the edge
of overcast eyes

wondering
if I should leap.

dinner dance

We do the banter ballet
beside the breadbasket –

then somewhere between
appetizers and entrees
I stop rehearsing.

When dessert arrives
with two forks,
I'm still pulling off
pirouettes –

and it seems
we're both ready
for our next movement.

first date

You opened up to me
blossoming
soft words
which I gently picked up
and tucked in my five-dollar purse.

I did not have to pluck your petals –
you let go of them like a dandelion
setting seeds free.

Then I found myself in the middle
of a tulip-tornado, surrounded by
pink stories, purple laughter,
smiles stimulated by photosynthesis.

I snatched the petals from the wind
with my butterfly net
and pressed them between the pages
of a story I haven't yet written.

careless/carefree

They catch me smiling
into my morning mug
of tea and nod –
they know
where I've been
and where
I'm going.

I sip and don't
say it, but
I know,
too –

I can see the clouds
convening in my cup,
the warmth's
inevitable
flight
back to morning –

I know where I am
and where we're going –
it's just,
for now,
I really don't
care.

scenic route

You're a distraction –
a scenic route picked
for pure procrastination,
but I'm shoving my responsibilities
to the bottom of my purse
with the gum wrappers, ChapSticks,
and unread receipts,
hoping
there's never a night
this all catches up to me.

t h a w

Who would've thought
a wink and some
well-placed wit
would be my undoing?

rendezvous

Meet me at the corner
of certainty and doubt
where right and wrong intersect.

We'll catch a cab to euphoria,
praying the traffic lights stay green,
ignoring the staccato shouts of stop signs.

We'll tuck crumpled maps
into our back pockets,
and roll down the windows
to laugh up at stars –
daring the universe to disrupt
our temporary permanence.

preservation

The moon rolls her eyes
while observing
our late-night conversations,
but for once, I'm not going to
condemn clichés –
I'll be your whiskey,
your wildfire,
your rose,
your rain,

I'll be anything –
as long as I can keep
these midnight memories
unscratched
by time.

three wishes

I hope this is more
than a pocketful of nights –

that our inside jokes
slide between the years,

we make millions
of moonlight moments,

and when I show you
the craters beneath the covers
you say something
that doesn't feel
unfinished.

the sound of you

Your voice is like the simile
I've been searching for.

I had to dig my way
through muddy clichés,
adverbs soaked in overuse,
and worn-out wordplay
to find you.

But then you appeared,
honeysuckle vines
spilling in spools
of green and gold
from your open mouth,
pouring out
the perfect words.

t r a j e c t o r y

You told me
three things
I never knew
about asteroids,
then three things
I never knew
about you –

I didn't think
collisions
could be anything
but chaotic,
and yet, somehow
your impact
has softened me.

storm chaser

I found you
in my darkest hour:

You stood in the center
of my hurricane
holding a candle,
urging me
to open my eyes
and call off the winds.

I reached for the confidence
hidden somewhere
behind cloud clusters,
inhaled the violent gusts
and silenced seas.

I stumbled,
but you caught my hand
and together
we searched
for dry land.

the thief

He stole my heart –
tucked it in his tuxedo pocket
then ran off toward the city,
leaving behind a trail
of silk petals
whispering for me
to follow.

the wanderers

There is a map tucked in his back pocket
and his lips twitch like an undecided compass
before he grins.

She's always had atlases
in place of irises,
stacks of packed bags
napping
in her closet.

She knows what it's like
to have a head covered in clouds,
to peer at pastel dreams
through an airplane window.

One day, he might ask her to run away.
One day, she might just say
yes.

daylight savings

September shrank –
but for the first time
I didn't have to face
an impending winter
alone.

multicolored envy

He said:
I'm jealous of that tie-dye blanket
you keep on your bed
because it gets to spend every night
wrapped around you
as you drift into lava-lamp dreams.

sidewalks in june

We walked through
your neighborhood
at dusk,
dodging sprinklers
and collecting
sidewalk stories –

the times before drivers' licenses,
when we were bike-bound,
whooping through the neighborhood at dusk,

the nights we came back home
after time away,
finding fireflies
on familiar flight paths,

the days we were still
summer strangers
giving glances
and wondering
what if.

driveway

We fell in love with the brake lights on –
and now all I ask
is that you turn off the GPS
and lift your foot from the pedal.

I promise I will help you
navigate the night.

theme park

He was afraid of heights and showing fear
so she held his hand on the rollercoaster
and pretended not to see him shut his eyes
as they freefell toward infinity.

b e a c h c o m b i n g

I didn't know there was something missing
        until I found you.

It was like stumbling upon an unshattered sand dollar
        after spending a lifetime collecting broken bits
        of sea glass.

We are a perfect accident
        brought together by the ebb and flow
        of fate's turquoise tides.

jetty days

You taste like summer –
salt and cherry Italian ice

eyebrows raised
like the peaks of waves
as you look at me,
your year-round
mermaid.

musings on muses

I find comfort in chaos.

I'm soothed by storms,
inspired by wildfires.

I dance during earthquakes –
sidestepping cracks,
sashaying through the rubble.

I dive into riptides
without plugging my nose
and meditate in crosswalks,
sitting crisscrossed and sipping tea
while pedestrians scurry around me like ants.

I tuck myself into a bed of nails
at the center of a roofless room
and say to the sky:

Perhaps it is love
that has placed me
in paths of peril.

Perhaps is love
that has made me
fearless.

intricacy

We met on a Tuesday
between the stacks of a secondhand bookstore –
I drank your presence like hot cocoa,
letting it fog my glasses.

On Wednesday we wandered
through a sunflower field
ignoring the storm clouds
huddling
on the horizon.

Now it rains some Sundays
while you leave me waiting
outside the bus stop
by the secondhand bookstore.

You arrive thirty-three minutes late
with a yellow umbrella
and a cup of hot cocoa.

With you, I've learned
love is both the blindfold
and the hands untying its knot.

game nights

I want you on my team
for Pictionary parties
or barbecue battles
of Capture the Flag.

And I think
you'll be a key player
even when we aren't
rolling dice
or running.

the theory of us

We feel so inevitable –
I'm confident we have transcended
the laws of physics
and found each other
in every parallel universe.

durability

We are perfect together
because we can be apart
without falling apart.

the pantry: top shelf

Everyone's been waiting
for our expiration date –
dying to get their grubby little hands
on our happiness,
to be the first one to witness
its rot.

They've already plugged their noses,
expecting to be greeted
by the stench of failure –
their cue to toss us out
with a triumphant
"I told you so."

Yet many years later
they'll still be waiting,
drooling and impatient
as we stand together
high above their heads
on a shelf marked
nonperishables.

small comforts

There are days
when I lose interest
in airplanes and birds
and anything
going up,
when sadness coats my throat
and steals my words.

And I am thankful
for the way you measure out
metaphors
like medicine
when I forget
to see the sky.

friday nights

You pick the movie,
I'll choose the chips.

We can find romance
in routine.

last wednesday

It was a burnt meatloaf kind of night –
we sat on the kitchen floor
surrounded by Chinese takeout boxes,
trying to master chopsticks;
we chased dumplings around our paper plates
making food figure-eights and sipping sodas
while we talked about Mars,
and decade documentaries
and the Great Emu War.

We stayed there long after
our tailbones started to get sore
and the sodas went flat,
wondering why
these messy moments
make the best
memories.

our talks

I get lost in you like a book –
spending hours rereading your lips
and analyzing your irises
until static
replaces background sound
and time
turns to amber.

idols and mortals

You worship my weirdness,
watching from your perch on the jetty
as I sneak up on schools of fish
and chat with hermit crabs
who've lost their way.

I wave for you to come,
but you shake your head.

You prefer to watch
as I crouch over tidal pools,
creating currents with a stick
I've picked up for poking things.

Something calls to me further down the beach
past the second seaweed clump
beyond the third jetty –
perhaps an uncracked conch
or a turquoise teardrop
of sea glass.

I wave for you to run,
but you shake your head.

You worship my weirdness,
watching me from afar,
trying to soak up
my divine secrets.

But I am not a goddess,
and I don't want to be one –
so please, don't worship me.

Just come with me,
run with me.

ending

night fear

My worst nightmare
would be finding out
you are just a dream.

atlantic

I loved him like the ocean –
falling for the way his surface sparkled
but fearing the unknowns
that rested
in his depths.

b r e a t h s

Sighs sit soft
like white sheets in winter.

I wait;
you wait.

For a moment, I swear I can see the thoughts
crawling out of your head,
but it's just a shift in the shadows.

You wait;
I wait.

Your eyes are tired like pillows –
I want to stroke your hair
until dreams drizzle down your eyelids
and your face doesn't fight
expression
the way it does
when you're awake.

I wait.
I wait.

nightstand notebook

I want to know if you're writing about me;
if I'm pressed between the pages somewhere
in your nightstand notebook,
all done up in rhyme,
dripping
in gold
metaphors.

I want to know if you're writing about me;
if I'm sitting in your stanzas,
perched between the lines,
peering through a persona
you've hatched from hyperbole.

I want to know if you're writing about me,
but I'm not sure which would be worse:
if you thought I wasn't worth the paper
or if you thought
I was.

premonition

When you kissed me
I wasn't thinking about the moon
up there, waiting for the day-old clouds
to tire of blocking her ocean view.

I wasn't wondering why the seagulls
were standing instead of flying,
forming feathered phalanxes
as they stared, unblinking,
ahead,
wondering
why it had been months
since anyone offered them a french fry.

I didn't notice the mist yanking at my flyaways,
laughing as it undid any order
I'd imposed upon my hair.

The clouds thickened like tension,
but the gulls stood their ground –
or perhaps they were too lost in thought
to run.

When you pulled me in,
I didn't consider how damp sand
would cling to my clearance-rack boots
like evidence –
spackling the black
with an obscene amount of obvious.

I just let the salt settle on my skin
like dusk
and hoped confidence was something
that could be contracted –
something that would leak from your lips

and linger
on the tip of my tongue
even after February
fled.

f o g

Our air is clouded with misunderstandings
and I am responsible
for a good portion of the pollution.

the knot

She was more in love with their future
than she was with him.

So she tied him to her wrist
with satin ribbon,
dragging him through the years
while he admired her handiwork.

Most nights
they only smiled at sunsets
because it meant
another day passed
without a hurricane.

projectiles and persistence

You shot down my dreams with stones thrown
from slingshots,
picked them off with precision –
steady breaths, one eye shut,
rocks plucked from a garden
conquered by weeds.

With well-aimed words
you struck down my plans –
my feet rooted themselves to the ground,
and I was forced to watch
flightless feathers falling.

But I'm rendered sightless by sun
so I'll stay a bit longer
and hope in time
you'll lose your aim.

urge

Sometimes I want to run away
but I can't decide
if I want to run
to you
or
from you.

follow the leader

I never understood
why lemmings follow
one another
off a cliff.

But then I met you –
butterscotch sentences,
question-mark eyes,
and a voice that the voiceless
seek in their sleep.

You can capture our hearts
with various variations
of a smile,
sink uncertainty
with a knowing nod
or a soft pat
on the back.

You can lead us off a cliff
and we'll never see it coming
because behind you
we feel
so, so warm.

stomach this

The chicken I ate last night didn't agree with me
and neither did you.

Sometimes I wish I weren't so acidic,
stuffed with words like a book,
bloated from sentences
I've swallowed too fast.

But I've found that I'm an enzyme
breaking down your peptides,
your pep-talks,
in a petri dish at our dinner table.

Sometimes, I eat Tums just for their taste.
I've picked all the pink ones out of the bottle,
and I'm not sure what color to move on to next

or if you'll pass through my system.

friendly fire

When you were younger you liked war games –
hunt the enemy, shoot to kill
then go inside for cherry popsicles.

I don't think you ever stopped playing –
you hunt for my weaknesses
hurl names at me like grenades
as I learn how to dodge friendly fire.

After, we always numb the pain
with something cool and sweet;
distracting our tongues
from their war crimes.

There are no treaties on the table –
we tiptoe away
from obvious resolutions.

You've dragged me into these war games
and now I'm convinced
that without them, we'd be boring
because popsicles taste twice as sweet
after the heat threatens
to take us out.

ashen evening

I prefer the scent
of blown-out candles.
I crave smoke
over sweetness.

sugar-free

She said:
I like my men like my coffee –
black-souled and bitter
with tongue-burning kisses
that leave you shaking,
grasping at the half-filled mug
for dear life
until you're left lonely,
but strangely awakened
to earth's everyday tragedies.

m e a s u r e d

I want to hear you say something new
something that makes me stop
in the middle of washing the dishes
leaving the knife, crusted red with dry sauce
balanced
on the edge of the sink.

I can predict your words
with an accuracy any weatherman would envy –
but I'm still waiting for you
to surprise me
with a blizzard
during the sun-stretched days
of June.

m u m m y

You sleep
and you are
stiff –
arms at your side
a pillow resting on your chest
like a white bouquet
on a corpse
in a casket.

I worry that you'll live like this –
rigid and unblinking,
never allowing yourself
        to curl for comfort,
never allowing yourself
        to hold the person lying next to you
        who shivers between the satin sheets
that will never be enough
        to keep her warm
        no matter how many layers of luxury
        you embalm her in.

a daydreamed dimension

It seems that you and I can't exist
in the real world,
at least
not as the entity
we.

So I'll keep us alive in my daydreams –
a place where confounding variables
can be ignored,
the laws of magnetism reversed,
and our inevitable combustion
delayed
as I keep us suspended
in a universe
made from
make believe.

another night

After we say goodbye,
skyscraper lights will continue
their routine interruptions
of darkness.

Subways will slide
through underground arteries.

And I will sit
at the edge of the city
awaiting
my shattering.

the fading

We didn't end in a sonic boom.

You slowly slipped away
like an echo eventually lost
in a canyon brimming with night

and somehow
that was worse.

endings

You've always preferred
sunsets to sunrises,
fall to spring,
endings
over beginnings.

I should've known
our slip beneath the horizon,
our golden decay,
was
inevitable.

b a r r e n

If only I could buy little packets
of the right thoughts
like seeds,
plant them in my mind
and watch them
take root
in the places
green should have been growing
all along.

I don't regret you,
but I wish I did.

favorites

I've never had a favorite flower
or a favorite book
or a favorite anything, really
except for you –
my favorite
mistake.

u n k n o w n s

Your silence
screams at me
from across this town.

Unknowns echo in my ear –

What if,
what if...

Their reverb,
your revenge.

rationalization

I've distorted my memory of you
into something shapeless and dark
a bundle of soundless screams swirling
through my cerebral cortex
churning away at truth
until I can justify
leaving you alone
on our sun-stained
island.

p a s s e d

There have been hundreds of sunsets
since the last time we spoke.

Thousands of new hellos
have been exchanged
and the calendar pages
flipbook,
          flipbook,
                    past us.

But no matter how many numbers,
how many moments and milestones
I try to stuff between us,
it feels like just yesterday
you were pressing secrets into my palms,
weaving fingers through the waves of my hair,
making plans that would never see the light
of a star-glazed night.

s p a c e

Tonight, the sky feels extra empty –
there are no stars
and there is no you
pointing out all the places
constellations
wait for us
to connect the dots.

absence

Absence is an abstract noun
because it's not an object
that I can smell or taste or hold.

But your absence defies the laws of language
because I can see it sitting
in front of an empty place setting.
I can hear its knowing silence
as I flip through the pages of books
without soaking in any sentences.

Your absence never tastes like takeout
or Doritos set aside
for movie marathons.
Your absence tastes like
distraction dinners –
elaborate entrées,
experiments stretched out over hours.

Your absence smells like
Scrubbing Bubbles
and Lavender Fields Lysol
because now
I have plenty of time
to keep up with the cleaning.

I strap your absence to my back,
carry it through my days,
and at night

when I'm unable to peel it off
I wish it really were
nothing more
than another
abstract noun.

invasion

I don't like when these memories
break down the door
and come crashing into my quiet places.

I could dig a moat around my room,
fill it with the contents
of half-empty bottles –
Perfumes. Hairsprays. Cleansers –
hoarded beneath my bed.

I could create a fortress of bookshelves –
Cabot and Fitzgerald.
Riordan and Vonnegut.
All standing guard
as I sharpen my shell collection
into spears.

But in the end, it wouldn't matter;
the recollections would ram through
everything.

They'd hurdle my cosmetic moat
like a pesky parking-lot puddle
unfazed by the strange combinations
of fragrances:
Warm vanilla. Papaya and passion fruit.
Pink cotton candy and rosebuds.

They'd break down my book barricades,

separating series from shelves,
tearing through sections once organized
by genre or color or size.

My weapons would be useless –
snatched then snapped
and kicked aside.

I'd find myself cornered,
curled up in my upholstered armchair
trembling
against the aloof fabric
waiting
for the thoughts to finally
do
me
in.

farsighted

I have created conversations,
endless dialogues
between the two of us,
wedging fictional words into my mind-crevices
during the quiet hours before sleep
while staring up at the stick-on stars
clinging to my ceiling
until they become glowing green blurs.

I guess making a wish on plastic isn't sufficient
because when I ran into you at the planetarium
all of my midnight conversations evaporated
into stardust,
leaving behind nothing
but a slight nod
that you didn't even see
because you were too busy
staring up at Venus
wondering why real life
is never as pretty as the pictures.

waste

You tore me apart
like junk mail –
a flyer shouting with large fonts
and bright colors
stuffed into an overflowing mailbox.

But I wasn't trying to trick you –
wasn't trying to force you
to buy into something
you didn't need.

The years have etched lines of loneliness
into your face
and your knuckles seem to be frozen,
permanently
white.

I know what it's like
to be surrounded by echoes –
to scream at nightmares
circling the ceilings,
creating centripetal storms
until morning.

We could have chased each other's demons
to the farthest corners
of the universe,
but instead
you were careless –

created litter
from my offerings,
dismissed me
into the wandering wind.

entertainment

You wanted byte-sized love –
just long enough to fill
the commercial break
while you waited for her
to come back around.

betrayal

You said we were in this together,
two twin trees reaching for sky
side by side, never blocking
each other's sun.

But you leaked lies into my soil,
fed me falsehoods, stole my fertilizer,
whispered wishes for my bark
to be stripped barren.

You forgot
we were in this together.

You forgot
we were friends first.

useless charms

I've learned not to bet on you
because no matter how many four-leaf clovers
I string around my neck
or face-up pennies
I find on the streets
the odds will never find it in their hearts
to favor the chance
that you might change.

enemies

I'd like to think that I'm too old for enemies
that the only hate left in my heart
is a small smudge of gray
but some days
some days
I can feel the pettiness climbing
back up my spine
sinking its talons into my shoulder blades
as it leans down
and whispers in my ear:

*Don't you want
to win?*

t a n t r u m s

It's a pity
how petty I've become –
going out of my way
to kick down your sandcastles
even though the ocean
would have gotten to them
eventually.

jealousy

I feed monsters
and wonder why
my nights
stay stuffed
with nightmares.

last word

Clenched teeth and fists –
I am a grudge-girl
refusing to let go
even though
you
already did.

peaches

I miss being a peach-person,
sweet, blushing, full.

Tell me
how to stop the rot.

Tell me
how to return
to orchard days
and fruitfulness.

h a b i t s

I waste my time
waiting
for weightless
apologies
when I should be
chasing
new
daydreams.

expectations

My expectations
and my reality
stand in opposite corners
of the room.

Time shakes her head
and laughs
at my lack
of learning.

dim

I'm fading fast –
losing the color
in my words,
forgetting
what it's like
to feel
bright.

r e s i g n a t i o n

I've resigned from the role
of designated optimist –

my rose-colored glasses
were always held together
with duct tape,
and the left lens finally

cracked.

lost interests

I didn't put my book down
when I glanced over and saw
your name light up on the screen.

I'm not a spiteful person,
just tired.

I don't like rereading my writing anymore,
the same way I don't like looking in the mirror.

You'll say the same things you always say,
repackaged and reprocessed,
compressed for the sake of time.

It used to help –
but I think my brain has built up a tolerance
to your particular strain
of poisonous positivity.

I'm not angry,
just tired.

Worn down and wondering
if you can ever truly win
a war against yourself.

reprieve

I want to lie on my back
and let the current carry me
for a while.

I want to watch the clouds chase each other
into different corners of the sky
see the leaves fly like freed kites
that never worry about the meaning
of "away."

I want to float –
I've been swimming so long
I think I've forgotten
where I'm trying
to go.

insomnia

The directionless dawn
and desperate dusk
keep me
lost
inside myself.

I spend my days daydreaming
and my nights wide awake
waiting for some kind of epiphany
to curl up next to me
and whisper in my ear.

m u f f l e d

I don't want to be silenced.
I don't want to be
the person knocking at the door
when the doorbell is broken
my drum drum drumming
drowned out
by surround-sound living rooms
and vacuum voices
humming to be heard
over all of the
busy.

rush hour

Today everything feels taxicab yellow –
loud and bright
with hours rushing by outside my window.

If I lean on the horn
will the world slow down for me?

Or will I be resented
for disrupting the normal noise?

Sometimes, I want to scream
at the rearview mirror,
but I don't think anyone
would hear me
if I ever bothered
to try.

beginning (again)

the drive home

The road
unravels in ribbons
ahead of me
as I drive away
from you.

I wink back
in response
to the stars,
allowing myself
a small
smile,
and thank them
for the gift.

h u s h e d

There was no fanfare –
no stage songs or denouement dances,
monologues or ovations.

But still –
even without an audience
it was a great escape.

s u b p l o t

I found you
between the pages of a book –
well, your fictional doppelganger
to be more exact,
and it turns out
you were just a decoy
to that protagonist
too.

s h e

She is more than just the sum of her features –
two tulip lips
plus a handful of sun-washed hair
do not equal her name.

You have made her into a daydream –
stripped the personality from her skin
like thin bark
from a birch tree.

There are a hundred mysteries
echoing in her crystal-ball eyes
that you choose not to dive for.

There are a hundred mysteries
beating in her chest
that you choose not to hear.

She is not a myth,
not an archetype –

She is
the beauty of dawn
and the knowledge
hidden beneath blinding colors.

She is
the moon
selecting sides to keep in darkness

allowing access only to those
who pass beyond the light
to search.

blank calendar

I'm not bookmarking
any more weekends
for you.

From here on out,
it's just me, the breeze,
possibilities, and sleep –

deep
and uninterrupted.

ventriloquism

My voice
is so different from yours –
I never should have let you
use my tongue to speak
for all those years.

onward

You infected me with your stagnation –
halted my evolution
with silencing stares
every time I tried to talk about
something of substance.

One day, I caught a glimpse of my reflection
in the water,
but I couldn't see myself clearly
through the pond scum.

It took a few years,
but I coaxed my current out of hiding
and let it carry me forward,
leaving you
standing in the shallows.

stepping into the light

You taught me how to hate myself,
and I'm still struggling
to untie all the knots you twisted
inside my stomach,
still struggling
to erase the red lines that slashed
through my written words
leaving them illegible and bleeding.

I must silence the voices that creep up
in the empty hours of night,
drumming self-doubt in a rhythm
that sticks in my brain long past
morning.

I will no longer sing your song.
Internalize those lightless lyrics.
Drink pools of tar
from your hands.

My lips are cracked
and my tongue burnt,
but I've begun to take timid sips
of cool water
and in time,
I will walk
unscorched
by your shadow.

sparks

I am not sorry
for following the fire
or ripping the extinguisher
from your ashy hands.

Without you,
I can rise.

Without you,
I will ignite.

flight

She kept all the letters you ever wrote –
smoothed away the folds and creases
and laid them between the pages
of an old history textbook –
the thickest thing she owned.

But now she doesn't care about wrinkles –
she plucks the papers from preservation
and folds them into a hundred paper airplanes
with crisp, white wings.

She stuffs them into a faded teal backpack
and then drops the textbook
into the second largest compartment
because she doesn't want to feel
like she's carrying nothing.

Tonight, at the top of a water tower
or a skyscraper, a cliff or canyon,
it will rain paper planes
and she will no longer hate the heaviness
of her history
strapped to her back.

exile

I'm banishing you
to the land of unfinished poems
with all my other failed metaphors
that aren't worth revising.

power

I buy my own flowers –
keep chrysanthemums and Christmases,
sunsets and small moments
to myself.

I will not wait on windowsills
for you,
do the plant-perch
until you come home.

I will not wait
for you
to make me a life
I never asked for.

m o o n

I'm slipping into a new month –
chasing muses that don't
mute me.

author

you scribbled down plans
for our future
and never let me read
over your shoulder

But now I know
how to write my own
story.

Now I know
I had the pen
all along.

r e s u r r e c t i o n

As plaster crumbles like conquered castles

and tornadoes of ash and dust
coat her world in a quiet gray

she brushes the destruction
from her knees

and
rises.

beginnings

Bring me
beginnings –
a dawn,
a daffodil,
and a sunrise,
all unfolding
in the same
breath.

awakening

One day I woke up
and realized I hated
who I'd become

and that was when
I first felt a twitch
in my paper wings.

radical self-acceptance

You once told me
that baths are disgusting
and you can't imagine why
anyone would sit
in their own filth
willingly.

But I think there's something freeing
that comes from the ability
to stay in the water
even after the white bubbles
and steam
flee.

It's not always about trying to get clean –
sometimes, we just need
to steep
without getting repulsed
by the parts of us
that have turned the water gray.

icarus

I am melting,
but I've decided
not to step away from the sun.

I was forced into this mold
by rough, red hands,
but it's time to let my wax liquefy
so I can reform
into the shape
I choose.

b o u n d l e s s

You can't bottle my breeze –
I was born to help broken-winged beetles
take flight.

breakaway

poetry does not have to rhyme –
you do not have to be
who they expect

ditch prescribed patterns

catch
        the
chaos
        of your creations

someday
you might find freedom
in free verse

architecture

Don't be ashamed of who you were
before.

To the untrained eye, foundations
never seem as beautiful
as the buildings that spring up
from them.

But without bedrock and beams,
we would all sink
into the earth
and no one would ever witness
the light
shining through
on a Sunday morning.

independence

My stomach
has stilled –
the butterflies
I've relied on to carry me
through the days
are nothing now but withered wings
and expired echoes.

It's okay.
It will be
okay –
I can still rise
and reach
champagne-stained skies
on my own.

arizona

She used to be a palm tree –
always bending
for someone else's
wind.

But now,
she summons her own sandstorms.

Now, they call her the cactus
because she hates hugs
and could spend a lifetime
lost in the desert
without getting lonely.

stargazer

Tonight, I looked up at the sky
and saw myself in the constellations.

palate

She prefers rich brownies to cake
because she finds fluff and airiness
absurd.

She takes her tea without milk or sugar
because she doesn't want the bitterness
muted.

She is always hungry for loud flavors –
headache-sweet icing,
tear-jerking hot sauce,
fries rolled in mountains of salt.

Each taste makes a tiny proclamation
on her tongue
and she is reminded
to appreciate her own natural ingredients
even when others try
to dilute them.

lessons in botany

Why do all metaphors
praise the wild
and curse the tamed?

Can't we admire both
the carefree hearts
of wildflowers
and the precision-driven minds
of bonsai trees?

I want to learn how to see
beyond simplicity –
I want to find my
reflection
in nature's nuances.

substance

These poets
would compare me
to wine or champagne.

But I've grown bored
of all the drunken grandeur,
the watered-down
metaphors
and empty bottles.

I am not pinot noir
or merlot,
chardonnay
or sauvignon blanc.

Give me a simile
that won't drown me,
an analogy
that won't reduce me
to bubbles
and breath.

clever crown

I only want to be a princess
if the dress comes with a matching
sword and pen,
both sharp as my tongue.

the writer

Sometimes, I feel the least alone
when I'm alone
creating characters from shadows
watching them fly around my ceiling
twirling and swirling in smooth circles
leaving trails of stories behind
before they leap out the window
throwing themselves into the night.

I gather up the dust
rub it between my fingers
and whisper the magic words –
then, I get to work.

beckoning

She had flowers in her hair
flowers in her heart
so if you're forgetting all the ways
that life is beautiful
go and find her –
she'll be somewhere in the forest
by the sea or in the garden
waiting for you
to come and see.

the sculptor

Art
endures.

And so
will
I.

forward

Box up your loneliness –
blanket it in a soft snow
of packing peanuts,
seal the lid
with tongues of tape.

Box up your loneliness –
you won't need it
where we're going.

acknowledgments

I would like to express my heartfelt gratitude to all the people who've helped make the publication of this book possible:

To my loving family, thank you for your unwavering support throughout my journey as an author. From an early age, you instilled in me a love of reading and writing, and that passion remains strong today. Your belief in my abilities and the examples you've set both professionally and personally have been a constant source of inspiration, and I'm very grateful for your love and encouragement.

To my wonderful friends, thank you for being there for me during the highs and lows of the creative process. Your insightful feedback has played a major role in shaping this collection, and I'm so grateful for your enduring support.

To my teachers and mentors, thank you for sharing your wisdom, knowledge, and passion. Your guidance has shaped me as both a writer and an individual. I am indebted to you for all the ways you've nurtured my craft.

To my dedicated editors, thank you for your meticulous attention to detail and invaluable feedback. Your keen insights and suggestions have not only enhanced the poems in this collection but have also fostered my growth as a writer.

To my talented cover designer, Islam Farid, thank you for capturing the essence of this collection through your beautiful artwork.

Finally, to Michelle Halket and everyone at Central Avenue, thank you for believing in my work and giving it a platform to reach a wider audience. Your commitment to supporting emerging voices in poetry is commendable, and I am honored to be a part of your publishing family.

To all those who have played a role, big or small, in the creation of this book, thank you. Your influence, support, and encouragement have been instrumental in bringing this collection to life.

If you enjoyed this book, please consider supporting me by:
- Leaving a brief review
- Recommending the book to a friend
- Sharing the book and any poems you like on your favorite social media platforms
- Adding the book to shelves on The StoryGraph or Goodreads

about the poet

Kristen Costello is a poet, speaker, and mental health advocate who lives in Central New Jersey (yes, it exists!). She is the author of two full-length collections: *Tidal Pools and Other Small Infinities* and *Grey Matters*. Her work explores themes such as love, loss, mental health, personal growth, and healing. When she's not writing, you can find her beachcombing, watching space documentaries, or buying more books than she can carry.

TikTok: @kristens_notebook_poetry
Instagram: @kristens_notebook
Facebook: @kristensnotebook

c r e d i t s

creative direction: Kristen Costello

editing: Beau Adler

developmental editing: Jessica Peirce

proofreading: Molly Winter

cover design: Islam Farid

interior design: Michelle Halket

publisher: Central Avenue Publishing

sales & distribution: IPG

foreign & audio rights: Linda Migalti,
Susan Schulman Literary Agency

central
avenue
PUBLISHING

Central Avenue is a home for fiction and poetry about
us at our worst — and best.

We are proud to have had many of our titles on
bestseller lists, go viral, win respected awards, endorsed
by literary heroes and celebrities, and enjoyed by
readers all over the world.

Learn more about how this independent press works,
our books, and our authors at the link below.